Techniques for Effective Delegation

# How to Delegate for the Growth and Performance of Your Team?

Techniques for Effective Delegation

## Legal Information

**Book Title:** How Delegation Develops Employee Skills

**Copyright:** All rights reserved. Reproduction of this book in e-book or paper form is strictly prohibited without the express written consent of the author, including in whole or in part in any form or manner.

**Author:** Dionisio Melo

**Publisher:** Independent Publication

**ISBN:** 9798334497283

**Year:** 2024

Techniques for Effective Delegation

# Table of Contents

**Introduction - 5**

**Chapter 1**
Delegate the Entire Task to One Person -7

**Chapter 2**
Select the Right Person to Delegate To -11

**Chapter 3**
Clearly Specify Your Preferred Outcomes - 15

**Chapter 4**
Delegate Responsibility and Authority - Assign the Task, Not the Method for Achieving It -20

**Chapter 5**
Ask the Person to Summarize and Describe the Task and Expected Outcomes for You - 24

**Chapter 6**
Obtain Non-Intrusive Progress Updates as the Project Moves Forward -28

# Techniques for Effective Delegation

**Chapter 7**
Keep Lines of Communication Open -32

**Chapter 8**
If You Are Not Satisfied with Progress, Don't Do the Task Yourself!-36

**Chapter 9**
Value and Reward the Person's Performance -40

**Epilogue- 44**

**About the Author- 47**

# Techniques for Effective Delegation

## Introduction

In the 16-hour "Effective Leadership" course I teach to many companies who want to develop leaders among their managers, task delegation is a critical skill for managers at any level.

Delegating involves working with a collaborator to set goals, giving them sufficient authority and responsibility to achieve those goals, often by providing them with 1) substantial freedom in deciding how the goals will be achieved, 2) resources to help them reach the goals, 3) an assessment of the quality of their effort and goal achievement, 4) addressing performance issues and/or rewarding their performance. Ultimately, the manager is responsible for achieving the goals, but chooses to achieve those goals by delegating the task to someone else.

Delegating is different from directing work. When work is directed, the manager is telling someone what to do and how to do

## Techniques for Effective Delegation

it. There is generally much less freedom in how the collaborator does the task, and it is also often much less participation and learning on the part of the collaborators.

Delegating can sometimes be a big challenge for new managers, they are worried about having to give up control or struggle to have confidence in the skills of others. Managers who can delegate effectively can free up a lot of their own time, help their direct reports cultivate experience in learning, and can develop their own leadership skills, skills that are fundamental to problem solving, goal achievement, and learning.

How can you delegate for the growth and performance of your collaborators? I suggest the following general steps for implementing delegation.

**Techniques for Effective Delegation**

# Chapter 1
# Delegate the Entire Task to One Person

Delegate the entire task to one person. In doing so, you are not only handing over a comprehensive responsibility but also fostering a work environment that values autonomy and confidence in the team's skills. This type of delegation has multiple benefits for both the individual and the organization as a whole.

First, when you assign a complete task to one person, you send a clear message of trust in their capabilities and judgment. This act of trust can be tremendously motivating. The person feels that they have the support and faith of their superiors, which can significantly increase their commitment and dedication to the work. This trust also allows the individual to develop greater self-confidence and a strong sense of responsibility. Knowing that the success of a task depends entirely on their efforts can drive the person to strive harder and be more proactive in problem-solving.

# Techniques for Effective Delegation

Additionally, by giving one-person total responsibility for a task, you are providing them with an opportunity to develop and demonstrate a variety of skills. From planning and organizing to execution and follow-up, the person has the chance to manage all facets of the task. This not only assists in their professional development but also allows for a clear identification of their strengths and areas for improvement. The experience gained from handling a task from beginning to end is invaluable and can prepare the person for roles with greater responsibility in the future.

For the manager, this approach also has significant advantages. By working with someone who has a complete understanding of the task, the manager can focus on providing strategic guidance and support rather than being involved in the day-to-day details. This allows for more efficient time management and better utilization of resources. Furthermore, the manager can evaluate the results more clearly and objectively, comparing them to what he or she would have expected if they had personally performed the task. This clarity

## Techniques for Effective Delegation

facilitates constructive and precise feedback and can help establish higher and clearer performance standards for the team.

Likewise, delegating the entire task to one person can lead to greater efficiency and consistency in work. When a single person is responsible for all stages of a task, there is less risk of misunderstandings and communication errors that can occur when multiple people are involved. The person can ensure that all parts of the task are aligned and integrate seamlessly, which can result in a higher quality final product.

This approach can also alleviate the manager's workload, allowing them to concentrate on other strategic tasks and on the overall supervision of the team. By delegating complete tasks, the manager can manage their time more effectively and focus on the development and implementation of long-term strategies, rather than the detailed management of daily work.

Finally, delegating an entire task to a single person can also foster a sense of belonging

## Techniques for Effective Delegation

and cohesion within the team. When team members feel trusted with important responsibilities and given the opportunity to contribute significantly, they tend to be more engaged and satisfied with their work. This can improve team morale and create a more positive and collaborative work environment.

Delegating the entire task to one person not only optimizes time and resource management but also promotes professional development, efficiency, and team cohesion. By fully trusting an individual's skills and providing them with the opportunity to handle a complete task, you are fostering a work environment that values autonomy, confidence, and growth.

# Chapter 2
# Select the Right Person to Delegate To

Selecting the right person to delegate to is crucial for the success of any delegated task. Assigning responsibility to the correct person can make the difference between the success and failure of the project. When assessing a person's skills and capabilities, it's important to consider not only their experience and technical expertise but also their soft skills, such as communication skills, responsibility, and the ability to work autonomously.

It's essential to conduct a thorough evaluation of the collaborator's technical skills. This involves verifying whether the person possesses the necessary knowledge and relevant prior experience to carry out the task. For example, if the task requires specific skills in software, it's crucial to ensure that the person has the necessary competence in that area. Additionally, prior experience in similar tasks can be a reliable

## Techniques for Effective Delegation

indicator that the person can handle the new responsibility effectively.

However, technical skills are not the only factor to consider. Soft skills, such as problem-solving abilities, adaptability, and the ability to work under pressure, are equally important. An individual who has technical skills but lacks the ability to manage stress or adapt to unexpected changes may struggle to complete the task successfully. Therefore, it's important to assess these skills through interviews, previous performance reviews, and feedback from other team members.

If during this assessment it is determined that the person does not possess all the necessary skills, consider the possibility of providing additional training. Training can be in the form of formal courses, workshops, or even on-the-job training. Investing in the development of the collaborator's skills will not only benefit the current task but will also improve the team's overall capabilities in the long term.

## Techniques for Effective Delegation

In some cases, there may be a need to reconsider delegating the task. If the initially selected person doesn't have the necessary competencies and there's no time or resources for training, it might be more efficient to delegate the task to another team member who already possesses the required skills. This decision should be made based on a fair and objective assessment of each team member's capabilities, ensuring that the selected person not only can meet the task requirements but also has the interest and motivation to do so.

It's also important to consider the collaborator's current workload. Delegating a task to a person who is already overloaded may not be the best option, as it can affect the quality of work and increase stress. It's essential to balance responsibilities and ensure that the person has the time and resources necessary to focus on the new task without compromising their other obligations.

Effective delegation also involves clear and continuous communication. Once the right person has been selected, it's crucial to set

## Techniques for Effective Delegation

clear expectations, provide detailed instructions, and maintain an open line of communication. This will ensure that the person fully understands the task and can seek guidance or support if needed.

Selecting the right person to delegate to involves a careful and comprehensive assessment of technical skills and soft competencies, consideration of the need for additional training, and an evaluation of the current workload. By taking these measures, you can ensure that the task is delegated to a capable and motivated individual, increasing the likelihood of project success and fostering a positive and productive work environment.

# Chapter 3
# Clearly Specify Your Preferred Results

Clearly specifying your preferred results is crucial for the success of any delegated task, as it provides a precise and detailed guide on what is expected to be achieved. Clarity in expected results not only facilitates the understanding of the final objective but also helps keep everyone on the same page, minimizing misunderstandings and increasing the likelihood of success.

Describe clearly the specific objectives expected to be achieved. For example, if the task is to increase sales, clearly indicate the expected percentage increase and the time frame within which this increase should be achieved. Detailing expectations in a concrete and measurable way helps the person understand exactly what is expected and how their performance will be evaluated. This can include quantitative goals, such as sales figures or delivery deadlines, as well as qualitative objectives,

## Techniques for Effective Delegation

like improving customer satisfaction or service quality.

Explain why these results are desired. Helping the person understand the importance and impact of the expected results can increase their motivation and commitment to the task. For instance, if the increase in sales is part of a broader strategy to expand the market and ensure the company's long-term sustainability, sharing this information can provide valuable context. Understanding the "why" behind the objectives can help the person see how their work contributes to the overall success of the organization, enhancing their sense of purpose and belonging.

Clearly establish when the results should be delivered. Providing a detailed and realistic timeline is essential to ensure the task is completed on time. This includes specific deadlines for each project phase, as well as the final delivery date. A well-defined schedule helps the person plan and prioritize their work effectively, ensuring all project stages are completed as planned. Additionally, setting intermediate

## Techniques for Effective Delegation

milestones can provide opportunities to assess progress and make adjustments if necessary.

Identify who else might assist the person. The task may require collaboration with other team members or different departments. Clearly indicate who these people are and how they can contribute to the task's success. Providing this information helps facilitate coordination and communication, ensuring that everyone involved understands their roles and responsibilities. Moreover, fostering a culture of collaboration can improve the overall efficiency and effectiveness of the team.

Specify the resources available to the person. Ensure the person knows what resources they have at their disposal to complete the task. This can include access to specific tools and technology, allocated budgets, necessary materials, and any other form of support they might need. Providing a detailed list of resources and how to access them can eliminate barriers and facilitate smoother progress on the task.

## Techniques for Effective Delegation

Additionally, it is important to be available to answer questions and provide further guidance if needed.

Allow the person to decide how to carry out the task. While it is crucial to specify the expected results clearly, it is also beneficial to give the person the autonomy to decide how to achieve those results. This freedom can foster creativity and innovation, allowing the collaborator to use their own skills and knowledge to find the best way to complete the task. However, ensure you are available to offer guidance and support if necessary, and maintain open communication to resolve any doubts or issues that may arise.

Finally, it is often best to write down this information. Documenting all details related to the expected results, timelines, available resources, and involved collaborators provides a clear and accessible reference for the person in charge of the task. This not only helps avoid misunderstandings but also provides a formal record that can be consulted at any time. Additionally, written documentation facilitates communication

## Techniques for Effective Delegation

and transparency, ensuring that everyone involved fully understands their roles and responsibilities.

Clearly specifying your preferred results involves providing a detailed description of the objectives, explaining the importance of the results, establishing a clear timeline, identifying potential collaborators, detailing available resources, and allowing autonomy in task execution. Documenting this information is key to ensuring clarity and success in task delegation.Clearly specifying your preferred results involves providing a detailed description of the objectives, explaining the importance of the results, establishing a clear timeline, identifying potential collaborators, detailing available resources, and allowing autonomy in task execution. Documenting this information is key to ensuring clarity and success in task delegation.

## Chapter 4
## Delegate Responsibility and Authority - Assign the Task, Not the Method for Achieving It

This principle is essential for fostering autonomy and creativity within the team. By allowing the person to complete the task in the way they choose, you give them the opportunity to use their own judgment and skills to achieve the desired outcomes. This autonomy not only improves motivation and commitment, but it can also lead to innovative and effective solutions that might not have been considered otherwise.

Let the person have strong input in the project completion date. Involving the collaborator in the planning of the schedule not only ensures that the deadline is realistic and achievable, but it also fosters a sense of ownership and responsibility for the task. By collaborating in defining the deadlines, the person will feel more committed to meeting the established dates and more motivated to manage their time efficiently. Additionally, this practice can help identify

## Techniques for Effective Delegation

potential obstacles and necessary adjustments at an early stage, allowing for more effective planning.

It's important to recognize that, in some cases, you might not even know how to carry out the task yourself, especially at higher levels of management. This should not be seen as a weakness, but rather as an opportunity to rely on the experience and skills of your team. Team members often have specialized knowledge and unique perspectives that can be crucial to the success of the task. By delegating responsibility and authority, you leverage this experience and foster a collaborative and respectful work environment.

Make sure you communicate to others in the organization that this person has the responsibility and authority to complete the task. Clarity in communication is fundamental to avoid conflicts and misunderstandings. Informing colleagues and other departments about who is in charge and what authority they have ensures that everyone is aware and respects the collaborator's decisions and actions. This

## Techniques for Effective Delegation

can also facilitate access to necessary resources and support from other team members, creating a more cohesive and collaborative environment.

By assigning the task and not the method for achieving it, you foster an environment of trust and empowerment. Collaborators feel valued and respected when they are given the freedom to use their own strategies and approaches. This not only improves team morale, but it can also result in greater efficiency and effectiveness in carrying out tasks. Individuals are more likely to be engaged and give their best when they feel they have control over how they perform their work.

This approach can also be beneficial for the professional development of team members. By facing the responsibility of making decisions and finding solutions on their own, collaborators can develop leadership, problem-solving, and critical thinking skills. These experiences can prepare them to assume roles with greater responsibility in the future and contribute to the long-term growth and success of the organization.

## Techniques for Effective Delegation

Delegating responsibility and authority involves allowing the person to complete the task in the way they choose, involving them in the planning of the deadlines, and communicating clearly their role and authority to others in the organization. This approach fosters autonomy, creativity, and commitment, while it can also result in innovative solutions and significant professional development for team members.

# Chapter 5
# Ask the Person to Summarize and Describe the Task and Expected Outcomes for You

This step is fundamental to ensuring that both the delegate and the delegator have a clear and shared understanding of what is expected. By requesting a summary, you are providing an opportunity to clarify any misunderstandings and confirm that the communication has been effective. However, it's crucial to approach this step with sensitivity to avoid making the person feel questioned or untrusted.

Explain to the delegate that you are requesting the summary to ensure that you are effectively describing the tasks and outcomes to the person, not necessarily to ensure that the person is listening. Making this clarification upfront helps establish a tone of collaboration and mutual respect. Emphasize that the purpose of the summary is twofold: first, to confirm that you have clearly communicated the objectives, and second, to identify any areas that might

## Techniques for Effective Delegation

require further clarification or additional details. This explanation can alleviate any sense of mistrust and foster an open and positive working atmosphere.

The practice of asking for a summary not only validates that the information has been understood correctly, but it also reinforces the delegate's responsibility and commitment. By verbalizing what is expected, the person is reaffirming their understanding and commitment to the task. This action can also help identify any aspects of the task that may have been misinterpreted or require more detail, allowing you to address these points before they begin working on the task.

Additionally, by requesting a summary, you are promoting two-way communication. This allows the delegate to express their thoughts, ask questions, and share any concerns they may have about the task. This interaction can provide valuable insights and perspectives that may not have been considered initially. It also creates an opportunity to adjust expectations and ensure that all necessary resources are

## Techniques for Effective Delegation

available and any potential barriers have been identified and addressed.

The process of summarizing also has psychological benefits. When a person repeats and describes what is expected of them, they are mentally reinforcing the objectives and details of the task. This act of repetition can help solidify the information in their memory, making it more likely that they will remember and fulfill the specified requirements.

Moreover, by adopting this approach, you are demonstrating thoughtful and considerate leadership. You are showing that you value clarity and accuracy in communication and that you are willing to invest time to ensure that everyone is aligned and understands their roles and responsibilities. This can improve team morale and foster a culture of transparency and collaboration.

Asking the person to summarize and describe the task and expected outcomes is an essential practice to ensure effective communication and shared understanding.

## Techniques for Effective Delegation

Explaining the purpose of this request in a way that is not perceived as a lack of trust is key to maintaining a positive working relationship. This practice not only validates the clarity of communication, but it also reinforces commitment, promotes accountability, and fosters a culture of transparency and collaboration.

## Chapter 6
## Obtain Non-Intrusive Progress Updates as the Project Moves Forward

Staying informed about a project's progress without being intrusive is essential for the success of delegation. This approach allows the manager to be aware of the project's development and offer support when needed, without micromanaging the delegate. The key is to find a balance between staying informed and respecting the collaborator's autonomy.

One effective way to obtain this information is to continue receiving weekly written status reports from the person. These reports should be brief but comprehensive, providing a clear overview of progress. A typical report should include three sections: what was done last week, what is planned for next week, and any potential issues that may arise. This format allows for consistent tracking of progress, identifies areas that may need attention, and plans for the next stages of the project.

## Techniques for Effective Delegation

Weekly reports serve as an efficient and structured communication tool. They allow the delegate to reflect on their work, assess their progress, and plan their future activities. At the same time, they provide the manager with an overview of the project's status without the need for constant interventions. This method helps maintain the delegate's motivation and focus, as it gives them a sense of responsibility and control over their work.

Regular meetings with the person that provide feedback are fundamental in delegation. These meetings should not be seen as an evaluation or inspection, but as an opportunity to provide support, solve problems, and offer guidance. Constructive feedback can help keep the delegate on track and motivated. These meetings should be scheduled in advance and be part of a regular routine, providing clear structure and expectations for both the manager and the delegate.

During these meetings, it's important to create an open and trusting atmosphere. The delegate should feel comfortable discussing

## Techniques for Effective Delegation

their progress, challenges, and any concerns they may have. Active listening and asking open-ended questions can help foster honest and effective communication. Additionally, these meetings can be an opportunity to acknowledge and celebrate accomplishments, which can boost morale and motivation.

In addition to written reports and regular meetings, it can be helpful to use project management tools. These tools allow for real-time tracking of progress, facilitate collaboration, and provide a centralized platform for communication and information sharing. Examples of these tools include software like Trello, Asana, or Microsoft Teams. These platforms can offer easy and constant access to project information without being intrusive.

It's also important to be flexible and adaptive in your approach. Each project and each person is different, so it's crucial to adjust your monitoring method according to the specific needs of the project and the delegate's preferences. Some collaborators may prefer more frequent meetings, while

## Techniques for Effective Delegation

others may feel more comfortable with a more autonomous approach. Adapting your approach to meet these needs can improve effectiveness and job satisfaction.

Obtaining non-intrusive progress updates as the project moves forward is crucial for the success of delegation. This can be achieved through weekly written reports, regular meetings to provide feedback, and the use of project management tools. Maintaining a balance between staying informed and respecting the delegate's autonomy, creating a trusting environment, and being flexible in your approach are key factors to ensure that the project is completed successfully and efficiently.

## Chapter 7
## Keep Lines of Communication Open

This principle is fundamental to the success of any delegated task. The key is to find a balance between being available to offer support and avoiding micromanagement. Keeping lines of communication open ensures that the person feels supported and has access to the necessary guidance without feeling stifled or controlled.

Don't hover over the person to monitor their performance. It's important to avoid the temptation of constantly overseeing every detail of the delegate's work. This approach can create a sense of distrust and diminish morale, as the collaborator may feel that their autonomy and capability are being questioned. Instead, trust the person's competence and allow them to make the necessary decisions to complete the task effectively.

However, it's crucial to be aware of what they are doing. While you shouldn't control every aspect of the work, you should stay

## Techniques for Effective Delegation

informed about progress and any potential problems. This can be achieved through non-intrusive methods, such as periodic progress reports, scheduled meetings, and the use of project management tools. Staying informed without being intrusive helps identify any obstacles early and provides an opportunity to offer support when needed.

Support the person by checking in with them as the task is being done. Foster an environment where the delegate feels comfortable seeking help and advice when they need it. Make it clear that you are available to answer questions, offer guidance, and provide additional resources. This creates a collaborative and supportive work environment, where the person knows they can count on your backing at any time.

To keep lines of communication open, it's helpful to establish clear and accessible communication channels. This can include regular meetings, emails, instant messaging, and online collaboration platforms. Ensure that these channels are always available and that the person knows how and when they can contact you. Accessibility and

## Techniques for Effective Delegation

availability are crucial for building an effective and trusting working relationship.

Additionally, it's important to encourage two-way communication. You should not only be available to provide support but also be willing to receive feedback from the delegate. Listening to their concerns, suggestions, and observations can offer valuable insights on how to improve the work process and the collaborative environment. This open and honest communication can strengthen the working relationship and improve the team's overall effectiveness.

Transparency in communication is also essential. Be clear and specific in your expectations, and ensure that the delegate fully understands the objectives and deadlines. Clarity in communication reduces the possibility of misunderstandings and ensures that everyone is aligned toward the same goal. Furthermore, offering constructive feedback regularly can help the delegate improve their performance and feel valued and motivated.

## Techniques for Effective Delegation

Keeping lines of communication open involves being available to offer support without micromanaging, staying informed about the project's progress, and fostering an environment where the delegate feels comfortable seeking help. Establishing clear communication channels, encouraging two-way communication, and being transparent and specific in your expectations are key factors to ensure effective and successful delegation.

## Chapter 8
## If You Are Not Satisfied with Progress, Don't Do the Task Yourself!

This principle is crucial for effective delegation and for the development of the delegate's autonomy and skills. When you face dissatisfaction with the progress of a delegated task, the solution is not to take the task on yourself, but to identify and address the root of the problem. Taking the task into your own hands can undermine the delegate's confidence and morale, and it can perpetuate an unnecessary dependence on leadership.

Continue working with the person to ensure that they perceive the task as their responsibility. It's essential to maintain the delegate's sense of responsibility and ownership over the task. This is achieved through open and honest communication, offering constructive feedback, and providing the necessary support to overcome obstacles. By doing so, you reinforce the delegate's confidence in their

## Techniques for Effective Delegation

ability to handle the task and foster an environment of continuous learning and growth.

Seek the cause of your dissatisfaction. Before taking any action, it's important to understand why you are dissatisfied with the progress. This involves analyzing various factors that might be contributing to the problem. A lack of effective communication can be a common cause of dissatisfaction. Ensure that expectations, deadlines, and objectives are clear and understood by both parties. If communication is lacking, work on improving it through regular meetings, progress reports, and constant feedback.

A lack of training can be another critical factor. Evaluate whether the delegate has the necessary skills and knowledge to complete the task. If you identify gaps in their training, provide the necessary resources and training opportunities for them to develop the required competencies. This not only improves performance on the current task but also contributes to the long-

## Techniques for Effective Delegation

term professional development of the collaborator.

Inadequate resources can be a significant obstacle. Ensure that the delegate has access to the necessary tools, materials, and support to perform the task effectively. This includes both tangible resources, such as technology and materials, and intangible resources, such as adequate time and guidance. If resources are insufficient, work to provide what is needed or adjust expectations and deadlines according to existing limitations.

The person's commitment can also influence the task's progress. If you perceive a lack of commitment, explore the possible reasons behind it. It can be helpful to have an open and honest conversation with the delegate to understand their motivations, challenges, and any concerns they may have. Fostering a positive work environment, where the delegate feels valued and motivated, can increase their commitment and dedication to the task.

## Techniques for Effective Delegation

If, after addressing these factors, progress remains unsatisfactory, consider other approaches. This could include reassigning the task to another more suitable person or adjusting the objectives and deadlines to make them more realistic and achievable. In any case, it's crucial to maintain a supportive and collaborative attitude, seeking solutions that benefit both the project and the delegate's development.

When you are not satisfied with the progress of a delegated task, don't take the task into your own hands. Instead, continue working with the delegate to ensure they maintain responsibility, and seek the cause of the dissatisfaction, whether it be a lack of communication, training, resources, or commitment. By addressing these factors constructively, you can improve project progress and foster a positive and productive work environment.

## Chapter 9
## Value and Reward the Person's Performance

Recognizing and valuing a collaborator's effort and achievements is essential to maintaining their motivation and commitment. Performance recognition is not only about offering tangible rewards but also about providing acknowledgment and appreciation for work well done. This creates a positive work environment and fosters a high-performance culture.

Evaluate the achievement of the desired outcomes rather than the methods used by the person. It's important to focus on the results achieved instead of the processes used to get there. This fosters creativity and innovation, allowing collaborators to use their own skills and approaches to meet objectives. By valuing outcomes, you give employees the freedom to find the best ways to do their work, which can lead to more efficient and effective solutions.

Address both performance successes and insufficient reward. It's crucial to

## Techniques for Effective Delegation

acknowledge both successes and areas that need improvement. When a collaborator achieves the desired outcomes, they should receive appropriate recognition. This can include public praise, thank-you notes, or more formal rewards such as bonuses or salary increases. Public recognition can be particularly powerful, as it not only values the individual, but it also serves as inspiration for others on the team.

To effectively value performance, establish clear and objective criteria for measuring success. These criteria should be aligned with the organization's overall objectives and be communicated clearly to collaborators from the beginning. This ensures that everyone understands what is expected of them and how their performance will be evaluated. Transparency in evaluation also helps avoid misunderstandings and promotes a sense of fairness and equity.

In addition to acknowledging successes, it's important to address areas where performance has been insufficient. This should be done constructively and with the

## Techniques for Effective Delegation

intention of helping the collaborator improve. Offer specific and helpful feedback on the areas that need development, and work with the collaborator to establish an action plan for improvement. This may include additional training, mentoring, or adjustments to job responsibilities.

Rewards also play a vital role in valuing performance. Tangible rewards, such as bonuses, salary increases, or additional days off, can be very effective in motivating employees. However, intangible rewards, such as verbal recognition, professional development opportunities, and challenging projects, are also extremely valuable. The key is to find a balance between tangible and intangible rewards and ensure that they are aligned with the organization's values and objectives.

Fostering a work environment where achievements are valued and rewarded creates a culture of recognition and motivation. Employees who feel valued and rewarded for their work tend to be more engaged, productive, and loyal to the

## Techniques for Effective Delegation

organization. Additionally, this can improve team morale and create a more positive and collaborative work environment.

Valuing and rewarding the person's performance involves evaluating the achievement of desired outcomes rather than the methods used, recognizing performance successes, and addressing insufficient areas. Establishing clear evaluation criteria, offering constructive feedback, and providing appropriate rewards are fundamental to maintaining the motivation and commitment of collaborators, fostering a positive and productive work environment.

Techniques for Effective Delegation

# Epilogue

Delegation is not just a technical skill; it's an art that requires understanding, trust, and communication. Throughout this book, we have explored various facets and strategies for delegating effectively, ensuring that both leaders and their teams can reach their full potential.

Delegating a complete task to one person not only transfers responsibility but also motivates and increases the delegate's confidence. Selecting the right person for the task involves carefully assessing their skills and capabilities, ensuring that they are well-equipped for the challenge. Clearly specifying your preferred outcomes is fundamental to setting clear expectations and providing a framework within which the delegate can operate with freedom and creativity.

Delegated responsibility should be accompanied by the necessary authority, allowing the person to complete the task in the way they see fit. Asking the delegate to summarize and describe the task and

## Techniques for Effective Delegation

expected outcomes ensures mutual understanding and strengthens communication. Maintaining a constant flow of non-intrusive information about the project's progress allows for effective monitoring without micromanagement, and keeping lines of communication open is crucial to supporting and guiding the delegate on their journey.

When progress does not meet expectations, the solution is not to take the task on yourself but to work with the delegate to identify and resolve the underlying issues, be it a lack of communication, training, resources, or commitment. Finally, valuing and rewarding performance, focusing on outcomes rather than methods, is essential for maintaining motivation and commitment.

The art of delegating is a delicate dance between granting freedom and providing support. It requires trust in the team's skills and clear and open communication. By mastering this art, leaders not only free up their own time to focus on strategic tasks but also empower their collaborators,

## Techniques for Effective Delegation

fostering an environment of continuous growth and development.

Effective delegation is a cornerstone of successful leadership. It allows us to build strong teams, foster innovation, and ensure that our organization can face any challenge with confidence and resilience. As we conclude this journey through the art of delegating, I hope you have gained new perspectives and tools to implement in your own leadership, creating a work environment where everyone can thrive and reach their full potential.

In conclusion, delegating is not merely a management technique, but a leadership philosophy that recognizes the value and capability of each team member. By embracing and refining delegation practices, we build more efficient, innovative, and cohesive organizations. As you progress on your leadership journey, remember that effective delegation not only benefits leaders but also empowers collaborators, creating a virtuous cycle of trust, growth, and shared success.

Techniques for Effective Delegation

# About the Author

Dionisio Melo has carved out a distinguished career through his tireless pursuit of genuinely effective sales strategies for the demanding Latin American market. His influence encompasses various dimensions of the sales realm, exerting a significant impact across the region.

He is not only a prominent speaker at sales conferences and an expert guide in personal training and coaching sessions for salespeople; he goes beyond by sharing his vast experience and novel sales strategies with a select group of clients.

In addition to his prominent role in the corporate world, Dionisio Melo has captured his profound knowledge in several books on sales and sales management. These publications reflect his commitment to sales excellence and his ability to address the specific challenges of diverse sectors.

Dionisio's impact as a sales expert is undeniable; his ideas and insights are

## Techniques for Effective Delegation

ubiquitous in companies from virtually every industry. His popularity transcends borders, reaching an audience of over 50,000 people through newsletters throughout Latin America. Moreover, his influential blog has been widely shared and republished on numerous websites specializing in business and sales.

Dionisio Melo continues to play a crucial role as an advisor to constantly growing companies, providing invaluable support for these companies to reach new levels of success in the competitive Latin American market. His dedication and commitment to sales excellence, backed by his valuable publications, solidify his position as an influential and respected figure in the region.

www.ingramcontent.com/pod-product-compliance
Lightning Source LLC
Chambersburg PA
CBHW072054230526
45479CB00010B/1057